Contents

Equipment
For general cake decorating

You will find the following list of general equipment useful when decorating cakes and cookies.

1 Cake boards
Drum – 12mm (½in) thick board to display cakes
Hardboard – a thin strong board, usually the same size as the cake, which is placed under cake to act as a barrier and to give stability to stacked cakes

2 Carving knife – a sharp long-bladed pastry knife, for levelling cakes and carving shapes

3 Cocktail sticks (toothpicks) – used as markers and to transfer small amounts of edible paste colour

4 Dowels – used in conjunction with hardboards to support tiered cakes

5 Measuring spoons – for accurate measurement of ingredients

6 Paintbrushes – a range of sizes is useful for stippling, painting and dusting

7 Paint palette – for mixing edible paste colours and dusts prior to painting and dusting

8 Rolling pin – for rolling out the different types of paste

9 Scissors – for cutting templates and trimming paste to shape

10 Set square – for accurate alignment

11 Spacers – 1.5mm (¹⁄₁₆in) and 5mm (³⁄₁₆in) for rolling out paste

12 Spirit level – to check dowels are vertical and tops of cakes are horizontal

13 Tins (pans) – for baking cakes ball, round and multi-sized

14 Non-stick work board – for rolling out pastes

15 Smoother – to give a smooth and even finish to sugarpaste

16 Sugar shaper and discs – to create pieces of uniformly shaped modelling paste

17 Modelling tools
Ball tool (FMM) – gives even indentations in paste and softens the edges of petals
Craft knife – for intricate cutting tasks
Cutting wheel (PME) – use instead of a knife to avoid dragging the paste
Dresden tool – to create markings on paste
Palette knife – for cutting paste and spreading royal icing
Quilting tool (PME) – for adding stitching lines
Scriber (PME) – for scribing around templates, popping air bubbles in paste and removing small sections of paste

Piping tubes (tips)

Also known as nozzles and pipes, there are many piping tubes to choose from, and which shape and size you select will depend on the medium you are using and the design of the piping you wish to create. Generally, however, the tubes used for buttercream tend to be much larger than those used for delicate royal iced details.

Tubes are manufactured from either plastics or metals such as nickel-plated brass and stainless steel. For best results, always use professional piping tubes and avoid ones with seams. If your budget allows, use stainless steel tubes where possible, as these do not rust or break and should last you a lifetime.

Also be aware that the number series used to identify piping tubes is not standardized so you'll find that each manufacturer has its own slightly different numbering system. For example a Wilton no. 10 equals a PME no. 16. Before using a tube, always ensure that it is thoroughly clean and dry, especially when using the very small ones.

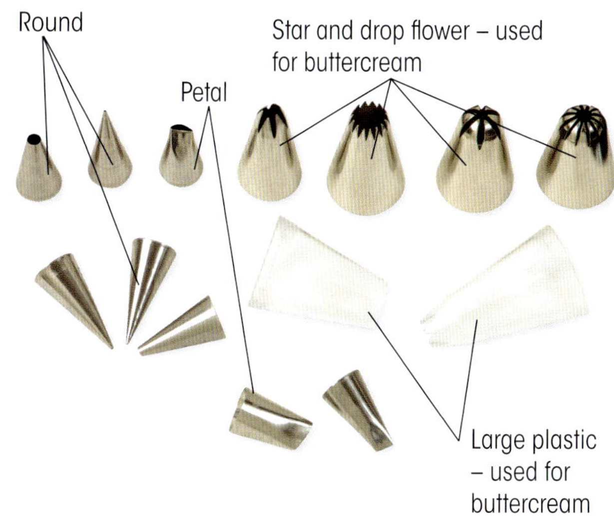

Piping (pastry) bags

These are available in two main types: reusable bags, now usually manufactured from proofed nylon rather than traditional cotton, which required boiling to sterilize, and disposable bags manufactured from clear plastic or greaseproof paper. I personally favour large plastic disposable bags for piping buttercream and small proofed nylon reusable bags for royal icing, however it is important for you to find out which you prefer. Many people also like to make their own greaseproof paper bags – the choice is yours.

Piping bag couplers

These clever devices are wonderful time savers; they are added into the end of piping (pastry) bags to enable tubes (tips) to be easily changed, thus removing the need to have a new piping bag for each tube.

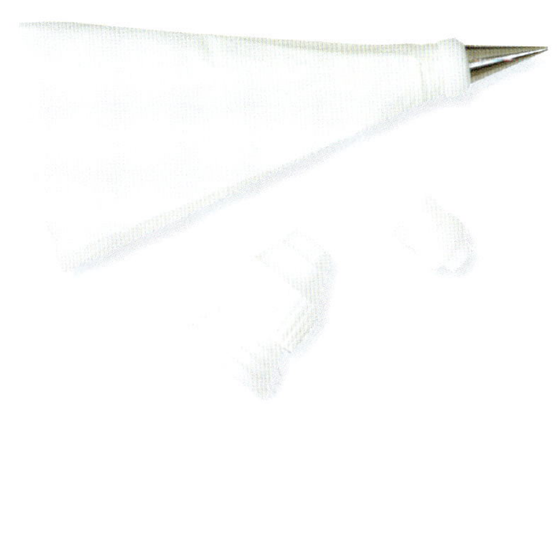

Sugar Recipes

Most of the sugar recipes used in this booklet for covering and decoration can easily be made at home. Use edible paste colours to colour them according to the individual project.

Sugarpaste (rolled fondant)

Used to cover cakes and boards, ready-made sugarpaste can be obtained from major supermarkets and cake-decorating suppliers, and is available in white and the whole colour spectrum. It is also easy and inexpensive to make your own.

Ingredients
Makes 1kg (2¼lb)

- ★ 60ml (4 tbsp) cold water
- ★ 20ml (4 tsp/1 sachet) powdered gelatine
- ★ 125ml (4 fl oz) liquid glucose
- ★ 15ml (1 tbsp) glycerine
- ★ 1kg (2¼lb) icing (confectioners') sugar, sifted, plus extra for dusting

1 Place the water in a small bowl, sprinkle over the gelatine and soak until spongy. Stand the bowl over a saucepan of hot but not boiling water and stir until the gelatine is dissolved. Add the glucose and glycerine, stirring until well blended and runny.

2 Put the sifted icing (confectioners') sugar in a large bowl. Make a well in the centre and slowly pour in the liquid ingredients, stirring constantly. Mix well.

3 Turn out onto a surface dusted with icing (confectioners') sugar and knead until smooth, sprinkling with extra sugar if the paste becomes too sticky. The paste can be used immediately or tightly wrapped and stored in a plastic bag until required.

Modelling paste

Used to add decoration to cakes, this versatile paste keeps its shape well and dries harder than sugarpaste. Although there are commercial pastes available, it is easy and a lot cheaper to make your own – I always do!

Ingredients
Makes 225g (8oz)

- ★ 225g (8oz) sugarpaste (rolled fondant)
- ★ 5ml (1 tsp) gum tragacanth

Make a well in the sugarpaste and add the gum tragacanth. Knead in. Wrap in a plastic bag and allow the gum to work before use. You will begin to feel a difference in the paste after an hour or so, but it is best left overnight. The modelling paste should be firm but pliable with a slight elastic texture. Kneading the modelling paste makes it warm and easy to work with.

tip...

For tips and discussion about making your own sugarpaste, visit the Lindy's Cakes blog.

Modelling paste tips

- ★ Gum tragacanth is a natural gum available from cake-decorating suppliers.
- ★ If time is short use CMC (Tylose) instead of gum tragacanth – this a synthetic alternative but it works almost straight away.
- ★ Placing your modelling paste in a microwave for a few seconds is an excellent way of warming it for use.
- ★ If you have previously added a large amount of colour to your paste and it is consequently too soft, an extra pinch or two of gum tragacanth will be necessary.
- ★ If your paste is crumbly or too hard to work, add a touch of white vegetable fat (shortening) and a little cooled boiled water and knead until softened.

Buttercream

Buttercream is used as a filling between layers of cake, as a glue to attach sugarpaste to cakes, and as a topping on cupcakes.

Standard buttercream

Ingredients
Makes 450g (1lb)

- 110g (3¾oz) unsalted (sweet) butter
- 350g (12oz) icing (confectioners') sugar
- 15–30ml (1–2 tbsp) milk or water
- A few drops of vanilla extract or alternative flavouring

1 Place the butter in a bowl and beat until light and fluffy.

2 Sift the icing (confectioners') sugar into the bowl and continue to beat until the mixture changes colour.

3 Add just enough milk or water to give a firm but spreadable consistency.

4 Flavour by adding the vanilla or alternative flavouring, then store the buttercream in an airtight container until required.

Flavouring buttercream

Try replacing the liquid in the recipes with:

- ★ Alcohols such as whisky, rum or brandy
- ★ Other liquids such as coffee, melted chocolate, lemon curd or fresh fruit purees
- ★ Or add:
- ★ Nut butters to make a praline flavour
- ★ Flavours such as mint or rose extract

Swiss meringue buttercream

For me, this is the best type of buttercream for cupcakes because it is less sweet and it has a beautiful glossy finish. However be warned, this buttercream is not stable above about 15°C (59°F), so it is not suitable for hot days or warm climates!

Ingredients
Makes 500g (1lb 1½oz)

- 4 large (US extra large) egg whites
- 250g (9oz) caster (superfine) sugar
- 250g (9oz) unsalted (sweet) butter, softened
- A few drops of vanilla extract

1 Place the egg whites and sugar in a bowl over a saucepan of simmering water. Stir to prevent the egg whites cooking.

2 Once the sugar crystals have dissolved, remove the bowl from the heat and whisk the meringue to its full volume and until the mixture is cool – about five minutes.

3 Add the butter and vanilla and continue to whisk for about 10 minutes. The mixture will reduce in volume and look curdled – don't panic, just keep whisking until the icing has a smooth, light and fluffy texture.

4 This buttercream is stable at a cool room temperature for a day or two. Store any unused buttercream in a refrigerator and re-beat before using.

Piping with buttercream

It is important that your buttercream is the correct consistency and temperature when using it for piping. If it is too stiff and cold it will be very difficult to pipe successfully, so you should re-beat it and add a little more water or milk. If it is too soft and warm it will not retain its shape, so chill it to cool it down then, if necessary, add a little more icing (confectioners') sugar and re-beat.

Pastillage

This paste is used to make sugar pieces that extend above or to the side of a cake and also to make sugarcraft moulds. It is an extremely useful paste because, unlike modelling paste, it sets extremely hard and is not affected by moisture the way other pastes are. However, the paste crusts quickly and is brittle once dry. You can buy it in a powdered form, to which you add water, but it is easy to make yourself.

Ingredients
Makes 350g (12oz)

- ★ 1 egg white
- ★ 300g (11oz) icing (confectioners') sugar, sifted
- ★ 10ml (2 tsp) gum tragacanth

1 Put the egg white into a large mixing bowl. Gradually add enough icing (confectioners') sugar until the mixture combines together into a ball. Mix in the gum tragacanth and then turn the paste out onto a work board or work surface and knead well.

2 Incorporate the remaining icing (confectioners') sugar into the pastillage to give a stiff paste. Store in a plastic bag placed in an airtight container in a refrigerator for up to one month.

Royal icing

Royal icing is used for piping fine details and for stencil work, as seen in some projects in this booklet. Below are recipes for two methods for making it.

Quick royal icing

This is a very quick method, which is ideal if time is short or you just wish to pipe a few details.

Ingredients

- ★ 1 large (US extra large) egg white
- ★ 250g (9oz) icing (confectioners') sugar, sifted

Put the egg white in a bowl, lightly beat to break it down then gradually beat in the icing sugar until the icing is glossy and forms soft peaks.

Professional royal icing

This is a more involved method that gives you a better quality of icing, ideal for piping finer details. Make sure all your equipment is spotless, as even small residues of grease will affect the icing.

Ingredients

- ★ 90g (3oz) egg white (approx 3 eggs or equivalent of dried albumen)
- ★ 455g (1lb) icing (confectioners') sugar, sifted
- ★ 5–7 drops of lemon juice (if using fresh eggs)

1 Separate the egg whites the day before needed, sieve through a fine sieve or tea strainer, cover and then place in a refrigerator to allow the egg white to strengthen.

2 Place the egg whites into the bowl of a mixer, stir in the icing (confectioners') sugar and add the lemon juice.

3 Using the whisk attachment, beat as slowly as possible for between 10 and 20 minutes until the icing reaches soft peaks. How long it takes will depend on your mixer. Take care not to over mix – test by lifting a little icing out of the bowl. If the icing forms a peak that bends over slightly, it is the correct consistency.

4 Store in an airtight container, cover the top surface with cling film (plastic wrap) and then a clean damp cloth to prevent the icing forming a crust, before adding the lid and placing in a refrigerator.

Piping with royal icing

The most important thing with royal icing is that the consistency of the icing is correct for the piping technique you wish to use. For the techniques in this booklet you will need both soft peak (normal) and smooth icing.

Soft peak (normal) royal icing: After beating your royal icing, make peaks in the icing with a palette knife and if the tips of the peaks bend over the consistency is correct; if not, re-beat until the correct consistency is achieved. This icing is used for drop line work.

Smooth royal icing: Paddle some soft peak icing on a non-stick board using the flat lower surface of palette knife to expel all the air bubbles. Then if necessary add a few drops of cooled boiled water to give a perfectly smooth icing. This icing is used for piping small shapes and for brushwork embroidery.

White vegetable fat (shortening)

This is a solid white vegetable fat (shortening) that is often known by a brand name: in the UK, Trex or White Flora; in South Africa, Holsum; in Australia, Copha; and in America, Crisco. These products are more or less interchangeable in cake making.

Sugar glue

You can often just use water to stick your sugar decorations to your cakes, however if you find you need something a little stronger try using sugar glue, which is a quick, easy, instant glue to make.

Break up pieces of white modelling paste into a small container and cover with boiling water. Stir until dissolved or to speed up the process place in a microwave for 10 seconds before stirring. This produces a thick strong glue, which can be easily thinned by adding some more cooled boiled water.

Piping gel

Piping gel is a multi-purpose transparent gel that is excellent for attaching sugarpaste to cookies. It also can add shimmering accents and colourful highlights. It is available commercially but is just as easy to make.

Ingredients

- ★ 30ml (2 tbsp) powdered gelatine
- ★ 30ml (2 tbsp) cold water
- ★ 500ml (18 fl oz) golden syrup (corn syrup)

Sprinkle the gelatine over the cold water in a small saucepan and leave to set for about five minutes. Heat on low until the gelatine has become clear and dissolved – do not boil. Add the syrup and stir thoroughly. Cool and store, refrigerated, for up to two months.

Rose Swirls

PIPING BUTTERCREAM SWIRLS
ON CUPCAKES

Practice makes perfect when creating this design – continue piping your buttercream swirls until you achieve seamless roses like these.

You will need

- ★ Cupcakes baked in brown and gold metallic high tea cases

- ★ Buttercream

- ★ Orange edible paste colour

- ★ Piping tube (tip): W – 2D

- ★ Large piping (pastry) bag

- ★ Basic equipment (see pages 2–3)

1 To create a simple rose swirl, place your star or drop flower tube (tip) into a large piping (pastry) bag then half fill the bag with buttercream. To create the two-tone rose swirls, add both orange and plain buttercream colours to the bag.

2 Once filled, twist the top of the bag to seal it. Hold the bag vertically slightly above the centre of the cupcake.

3 Apply pressure to the bag, then move the tube to the edge of the cake and go around the centre in an anticlockwise (counter-clockwise) direction, holding the tube above the cake surface so the icing falls into place.

4 To complete this simple rose design, release the pressure and remove the piping bag when you have completed one full circle.

Variation

Alternatively continue piping by adding one or two smaller circles of buttercream on top of the first.

tip...
I suggest you try experimenting with different piping tubes, as you will achieve different effects with quite similar looking tubes.

Peaks of Perfection

PIPING BUTTERCREAM PEAKS ON CUPCAKES

Peaks of piped buttercream make the ideal basis for these cupcakes topped with small moulded flowers and red pastillage rope-effect flourishes.

You will need

★ Cupcakes baked in black paper cases

★ Buttercream

★ Piping tube (tip): W – 1E

★ Large piping (pastry) bag

★ Modelling paste: red, orange

★ Pastillage: red

★ Silicone daisy mould (FI – FL288)

★ Sugar shaper

★ Rope tube (tip): PME no. 42

★ Basic equipment (see pages 2–3) cutter, same size as cupcakes

★ Basic equipment (see pages 2–3)

1 First create a red pastillage shape for your rope-effect flourish using the sugar shaper fitted with the rope disc (see page 29). Shape as desired then allow to dry.

2 Place your chosen tube (tip) into a large piping (pastry) bag then half fill the bag with buttercream. Twist the top of the bag to seal it. Hold the bag vertically slightly above the centre of the cupcake. Keeping the bag still, apply continuous pressure and allow the icing to spread towards the edge of the cupcake.

3 Once the buttercream has spread, slowly start to lift the bag while maintaining an even pressure. Release the pressure once the desired height has been reached and remove the bag.

4 To complete the design, insert the pastillage piece and top your cupcake with a two-colour moulded flower made with the daisy mould.

Variation 1

An alternative to step 3 is to rotate the cupcake in your hand while lifting the bag – this adds a subtle twist to the pattern in the icing.

Variation 2

Alternatively, rather than piping one large peak, use the same tube to pipe lots of small stars/ flowers by applying pressure for only a short time before removing the tube.

tip...

This technique works best with more rather than less points/petals on the piping tube (tip). So I suggest you try experimenting with large tubes with at least eight points/petals.

Divine Daisies

PIPING BUTTERCREAM DAISIES
ON CUPCAKES

This very pretty technique for creating daisies with buttercream will quickly transform a cupcake. The beautiful piped daisies you create will need nothing more than a ball of sugarpaste in the centre to complete the look.

You will need

★ Cupcakes baked in pink and gold metallic high tea cases

★ Buttercream

★ Piping tube (tip): PME leaf or petal

★ Large piping (pastry) bag

★ Sugarpaste: pink

★ Basic equipment (see pages 2–3)

1 Place your chosen petal or leaf tube (tip) into a large piping (pastry) bag and half fill with buttercream. Twist the top of the bag to seal it.

2 Starting at the centre of a cupcake, hold the bag so the thick section of the tube is pointing inwards and the thin section outwards. Start squeezing the bag and draw it out towards the edge then back in to the centre of the cake.

3 Repeat, using even pressure for each petal, turning the cupcake in your hand as you pipe.

4 Add a second layer, making the petals shorter and then, if desired, add a third or fourth layer. How many layers you chose to add will be determined by the size of your cupcake and the size of your tube.

5 To complete your design, top with a ball of pink sugarpaste.

tip...

If your buttercream gets too warm and starts to melt as
it comes out of the tube (tip), place the bag in the fridge
for five minutes.

Vintage Roses

A full rose bloom makes
the ultimate cupcake
decoration and is
delicious when created
with piped buttercream,
as shown here.

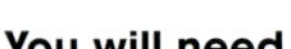

You will need

- ★ Cupcakes baked
  in blue and silver
  metallic high tea
  cases

- ★ Cellophane or
  waxed paper
  squares

- ★ Icing nail

- ★ Buttercream

- ★ Piping tube (tip): W
  – 103

- ★ Large piping (pastry)
  bag

- ★ Pink paste food
  colour

- ★ Basic equipment
  (see pages 2–3)

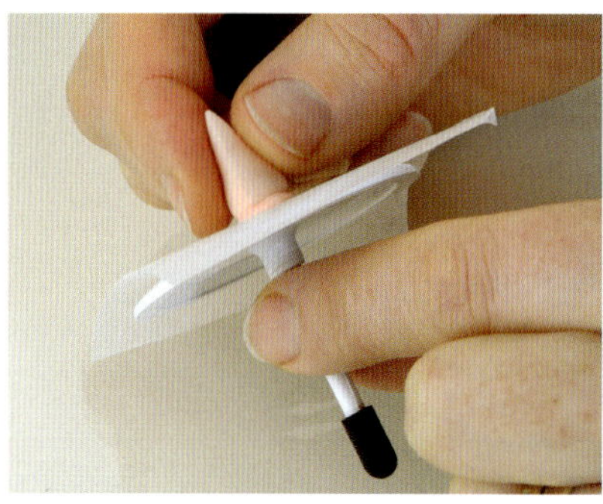

1 Cut small squares of cellophane or waxed paper and attach one to the top of your icing nail with a little buttercream. The first stage is to make a cone of a suitable size – you can pipe this with buttercream, but I have found that making cones from sugarpaste gives a firmer centre to the roses. Attach or pipe a cone to the centre of the icing nail.

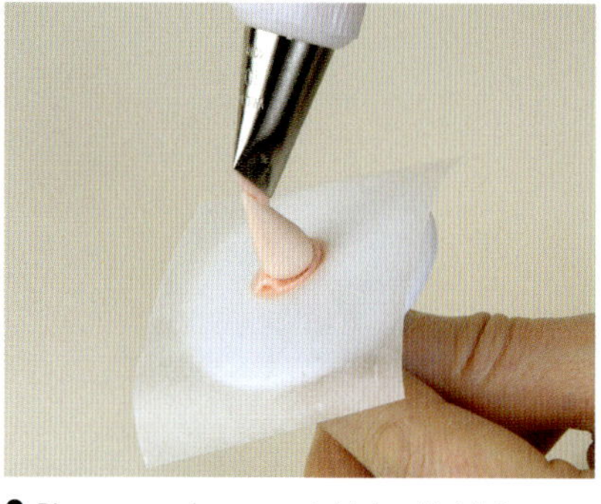

2 Place your chosen petal tube (tip) into a large piping (pastry) bag and half fill with the pink buttercream. Position the tube at right angles to the nail with the wider end of the tube at the bottom and the thinner end at the top. Raise the tube up so that the tip of the cone is halfway up the tube. You are now ready to start piping.

3 Start squeezing the bag, turning the nail as you pipe to create the tight coiled centre of the rose, about one and a half times around.

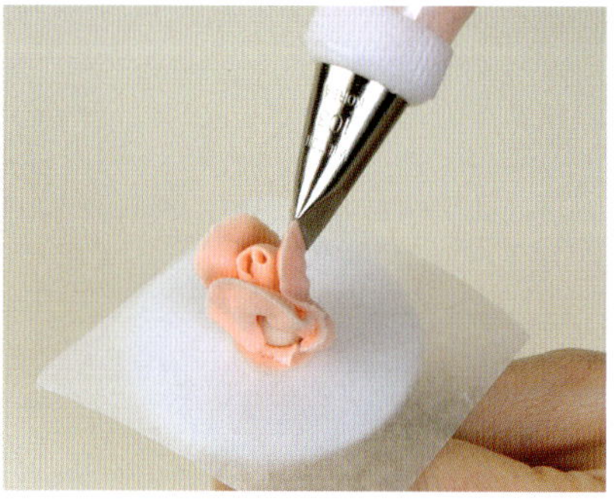

4 Keeping the nail upright, add three interlocking petals around the centre. Start at the base of the cone and apply pressure to the bag, lifting the tube up to the top of the centre and then drop back to the base to create the first petal. Pipe two more to complete the circle.

5 Add the next row of rose petals, making these more open by tilting the nail not the tube, this time adding five petals in the row. Continue adding as many rows of petals as desired, increasing the number of petals in each row by two each time.

6 Slip the cellophane or waxed paper square from the nail and leave the piped rose to dry. Once the rose has dried sufficiently to be handled, carefully remove the protective square and add the rose to the top of your cupcake.

tip...

The techniques for piping buttercream and royal icing are the same
— it is the scale that is different. If you wish to pipe a small rose
rather than a large buttercream one, simply use a smaller petal
tube (tip) and royal icing instead.

Whole Lotta Dots

PIPING ROYAL ICING DOTS ON COOKIES

You will need

- ★ Heart and pram cookies and cutters (LC)

- ★ Sugarpaste: teal, light teal, pink, flesh

- ★ Modelling paste: pink, dark brown

- ★ Piping tubes (tips): PME no. 1, 1.5, 2

- ★ Modern flowers stencil (DS – C559)

- ★ Cutters: set of round pastry cutters, daisy marguerites (PME)

- ★ Royal icing

- ★ Superwhite dust (SF)

- ★ Teal edible paste colour

- ★ Piping (pastry) bag and coupler

- ★ Basic equipment (see pages 2–3)

1 Stencil freshly rolled-out sugarpaste using the modern flowers stencils and appropriately coloured royal icing (full instructions on how to do this can be found in *The Contemporary Cake Decorating Bible – Stencilling* booklet).

2 Cut out hearts and sections of the pram from the sugarpaste using the heart and pram cutters then add to the cookies before the royal icing sets.

3 Add light teal sugarpaste wheels to the pram, using the round pastry cutters to cut these out, and a handle. Indent each wheel with a slightly smaller circle.

4 Using the flesh sugarpaste, cut and add a circle for the baby's head, then add a smile using the wide end of a piping tube (tip) and add eyes with a cocktail stick (toothpick). Model a curl of brown modelling paste for hair and cut pink modelling paste flowers for the wheel spokes.

5 To add the piped royal icing dots to your design, place a small round tube (tip), e.g. PME no. 1 or 2, into a small piping (pastry) bag and half fill with freshly paddled smooth royal icing.

6 Supporting your hand, either on your work surface or turntable, or with your other hand, hold the tube fractionally above the surface on which you wish to pipe.

7 Squeeze the bag until the dot is the required size, release the pressure and only then remove the tube – this helps avoid any unwanted peaks. Remember: squeeze, release and lift.

Fresh icing is always better than old icing for piping as it
holds its shape, is stiffer and is therefore easier to control.

Lovely Lace

Drop line work was used to link the floral motifs of this mini-cake, transforming it into a lace-effect design.

You will need

- ★ 6cm (2.5in) mini-cake

- ★ Sugarpaste: purple

- ★ Modelling paste: white

- ★ Piping tube (tip): PME no. 1

- ★ Piping (pastry) bag

- ★ Royal icing

- ★ Cutters: curled leaf set (LC), flame set (LC), flat florals (LC), Indian scroll (LC), small teardrop (LC)

- ★ Superwhite dust (SF)

- ★ Basic equipment (see pages 2–3)

1 Cover the mini-cake with purple sugarpaste and allow to dry (see page 29). Cut out shapes from thinly rolled-out white modelling paste using the various cutters and attach to the cake as desired, leaving enough space to add the piped details.

2 To pipe the lace threads, follow the technique that has been demonstrated here on a board. Place a small round tube (tip), e.g. PME no. 1, into a small piping (pastry) bag and half fill with freshly beaten soft peak royal icing. Hold the bag with your forefinger pointing down the front ready to apply pressure with only your thumb.

3 Touch the surface where your line is to start with the tip of the tube and at the same time lightly apply pressure to the bag. As the icing starts to come out, lift the tube up from the cake so it is at least 4cm (1½in) above the sugarpaste surface.

4 When the icing is of the length you need, release the pressure and place the icing down onto the surface of the cake. Remember: touch, lift and place. Continue to link the cut-outs with these threads until complete and finish by piping royal icing dots around your design, as shown on page 16.

tip...

To avoid lines breaking, don't use your bag for more than
15–20 minutes, as your hands will make the icing too warm.
Always re-beat your icing before starting again.

Monochrome Mugs

PIPING ROYAL ICING BRUSHWORK
EMBROIDERY ON COOKIES

A damp brush is all that's needed to turn a piped design into a brushwork embroidery masterpiece. For the most striking effects, choose either dark sugarpaste and light icing as shown in this project, or the converse.

You will need

★ Mug cookies and cutters (LC)

★ Sugarpaste: black, white

★ Art Nouveau tulip embosser (PC)

★ Craft knife

★ Royal icing

★ Piping tube (tip): PME no. 2

★ Piping (pastry) bags

★ Superwhite dust (SF)

★ Black edible paste colour

★ Basic equipment (see pages 2–3)

1 The first stage is to emboss or scribe a design onto your cake or cookie. The quickest method is to use the ready-made tulip embosser on your soft black or white sugarpaste, as shown. However, if you wish to create a unique design, scribe your chosen design onto your cake (once the sugarpaste has set) with a scriber needle.

2 Cut out mug shapes from the sugarpaste using the mug cutters and attach them to your mug cookies (see page 30). Place the small round piping tube (tip) into a piping (pastry) bag and half fill with freshly prepared smooth royal icing. For most shapes you need to work from the background to the foreground, so choose a small section at the back of your design and pipe around the outer section only.

3 Dampen a reasonably firm brush of a suitable size with cooled boiled water, blotting off any excess moisture with a paper towel. Place the brush on the wet icing and draw the icing towards the centre of the design with long strokes to give the design a natural feel.

4 When brushing through the icing, aim to keep the outer line unbroken, but you can always add more icing if necessary. Continue working around your design, brushing each section as soon as you have piped it to prevent the icing from drying out, until complete.

tip...

While you are perfecting this technique, add a little piping gel
to the royal icing to slow down the drying process, giving you
more time to work on your design.

Baby Booties

PIPING ROYAL ICING HEARTS
ON COOKIES

Piping hearts on top of
sugarpaste hearts creates
a charming layered
effect on these delightful
cookies.

You will need

★ Baby sock cookies
  and cutters (LC)

★ Sugarpaste: pink

★ Modelling paste:
  dark pink

★ Palette knife

★ Quilting tool (PME)

★ Small heart plunger
  cutters (PME)

★ Royal icing

★ Piping tube (tip):
  PME no. 1

★ Piping (pastry) bag

★ Superwhite dust (SF)

★ Basic equipment
  (see pages 2–3)

1 Cut out socks from the pink sugarpaste using the baby sock cutters. Cut away the tops of the socks and add vertical lines using a palette knife.

2 Attach both sections of the socks to the baby sock cookies (see page 30) then define the toe and heel sections with the quilting tool. Add a selection of small hearts cut with small heart plunger cutters from dark pink modelling paste.

3 To create the piped hearts, first pipe a dot using whitened smooth royal icing, but rather than removing the tube (tip), pull it through the centre of the dot to create a teardrop shape before removing.

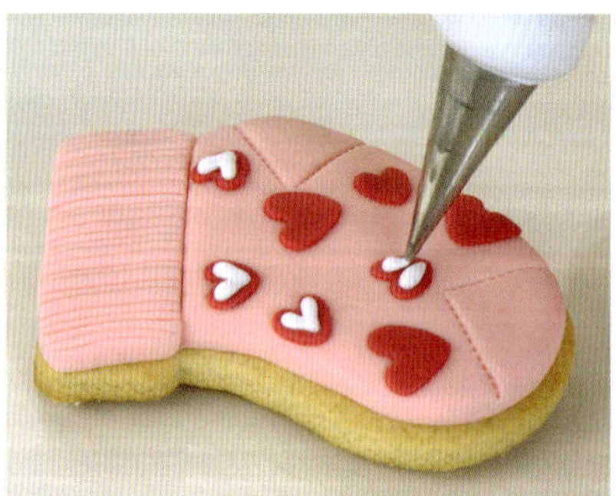

4 Pipe a second dot close to the top of the first teardrop, then pull the tube through the centre to meet the narrow end of the first teardrop to create a heart shape.

5 To complete the design, pipe dots as required, following the instructions on page 16.

Coral Creation

YOUR PIPED MASTERPIECE!

Piping results in a wealth of different effects – brushwork embroidery and piped dots feature on this amazing tiered creation, which has been created using techniques demonstrated throughout this booklet.

You will need

★ Round cakes: 18cm (7in), 10cm (4in)

★ Round cake drums: 28cm (11in), 20cm (8in), 12.5cm (5in)

★ Template (see page 25)

★ Sugarpaste: 800g (1¾lb) each dark coral, mid coral, 500g (1lb 2oz) white with a touch of coral, 400g (14oz) light coral

★ Modelling paste: 25g (1oz) of all four sugarpaste colours

★ Piping tubes (tips): PME no. 1, 2, 16

★ Reusable piping (pastry) bag and coupler

★ Royal icing

★ Superwhite dust (SF)

★ Sugar shaper

★ 15mm (½in) wide coral ribbon

★ Basic equipment (see pages 2–3)

1 Cover the cakes and cake drums with dark, mid and light coral sugarpaste, bringing this cover over the sides of the two smaller cake drums (see page 28).

3 Add a little superwhite dust to the royal icing and use to brushwork embroider the flowers (see page 20).

4 Dowel the large cake and stack the cakes.

5 Thinly roll out the white modelling paste and cut out circles with the no. 16 piping tube (tip) (see box overleaf) then arrange these randomly over the stacked cake.

2 Using the template on page 25, emboss or scribe flowers onto the cakes and largest board (see box). Note – the method you use will determine if the sugarpaste has to be soft or crusted over.

Using a scriber

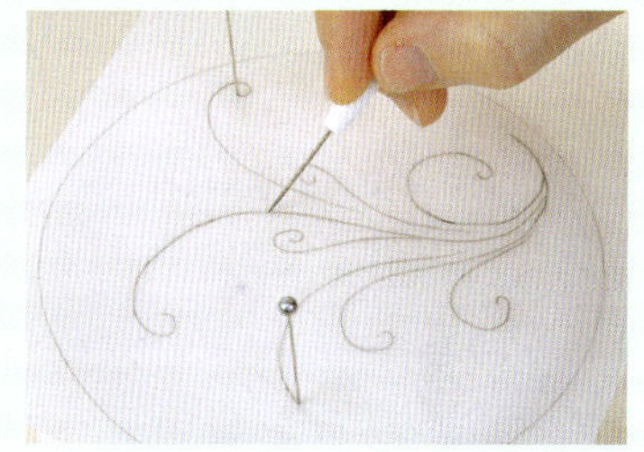

1 Trace your design onto wax parchment paper and pin or hold the design onto the cake. Trace the scriber over all the lines on the design, with enough pressure to mark the sugarpaste surface of the cake below.

2 Carefully remove the paper, the design should now appear as a faint outline.

Making your own embosser

1 Place a piece of acrylic that has been washed and sterilized with boiling water over your design then secure it in place with tape or a few dots of royal icing. Place a fine piping tube (tip) e.g. PME no. 1 in the piping (pastry) bag and half fill with fresh royal icing that has been paddled to a smooth consistency. Then pipe over the outline of the design.

2 Allow the icing to dry overnight in a warm, dry place. Once dry, position the embosser centrally over a freshly covered board or cake and press down firmly and evenly.

3 Remove the embosser to reveal the embossed pattern.

Creating cut-out shapes with piping tubes (tips)

These can make excellent small cutters – I find the plain round ones particularly useful. Place your selected tube on your forefinger and use as a cutter by pressing into freshly rolled out modeling paste. If the paste is picked up by the tube, use a soft paintbrush to push it out.

Template shown at full size. Download a printable PDF at: http://ideas.stitchcraftcreate.co.uk/patterns

6 Pipe small dots of royal icing around each circle and in the centres of the flowers using a no. 1 piping tube (tip).

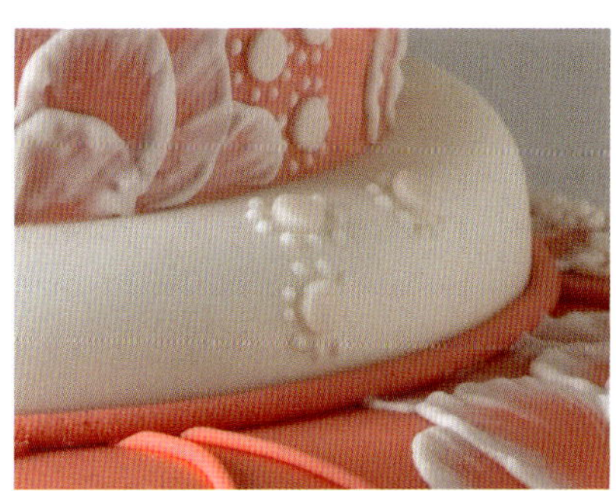

7 Fit the medium sized round disc into the sugar shaper (see page 29) and add trim of the appropriate colour to the base of the two smaller drums.

8 Change to the small round disc and add curved lines to the cakes.

Covering Cakes and Boards

Follow these techniques to achieve a neat and professional appearance to your cakes, cupcakes, cookies and cake boards. With care and practice, you will soon find that you have a perfectly smooth finish.

Levelling the cake

Making an accurate cake base is an important part of creating your masterpiece. There are two ways to do this, depending on the cake:

Method 1 Place a set square up against the edge of the cake and, with a sharp knife, mark a line around the top of the cake at the required height: 7–7.5cm (2¾–3in). With a large serrated knife cut around the marked line and across the cake to remove the domed crust.

Method 2 Place a cake board into the base of the tin (pan) in which the cake was baked so that when the cake is placed on top, the outer edge of the cake will be level with the tin, and the dome will protrude above. Take a long, sharp knife and cut the dome from the cake, keeping the knife against the tin. This will ensure the cake is completely level.

Sugarpaste quantities

Cake sizes		Sugarpaste quantities – 5mm (³⁄₁₆in) thickness
Round	Square	
7.5cm (3in)		275g (10oz)
10cm (4in)	7.5cm (3in)	350g (12oz)
12.5cm (5in)	10cm (4in)	425g (15oz)
15cm (6in)	12.5cm (5in)	500g (1lb 2oz)
18cm (7in)	15cm (6in)	750g (1lb 10oz)
20cm (8in)	18cm (7in)	900g (2lb)
23cm (9in)	20cm (8in)	1kg (2¼lb)
25.5cm (10in)	23cm (9in)	1.25kg (2¾lb)
28cm (11in)	25.5cm (10in)	1.5kg (3lb)
30cm (12in)	28cm (11in)	1.75kg (3¾lb)
33cm (13in)	30cm (12in)	2kg (4½lb)
35.5cm (14in)	33cm (13in)	2.25kg (4lb 15oz)

Note: These are the amounts of sugarpaste you will need to cover one cake, if you are covering more than one then you will need less than the amounts for each cake added together, as you will be able to reuse the trimmings.

Covering a cake with sugarpaste

1 For a fruit cake, moisten the surface of the marzipan with an even coating of clear spirit, such as gin or vodka, to prevent air bubbles forming under the sugarpaste. For sponge cakes, place the cake on a hardboard cake board the same size as the cake and place on waxed paper. Cover the cake with a thin layer of buttercream to fill in any holes and help the sugarpaste stick to the surface of the cake.

2 Knead the sugarpaste until warm and pliable. Roll out on a surface lightly smeared with white vegetable fat (shortening) rather than icing (confectioners') sugar – fat works well, and you don't have the problems of icing sugar drying out or marking the sugarpaste. Roll out the paste to a depth of 5mm (³⁄₁₆in) using spacers to ensure an even thickness (**A**).

3 Lift the paste carefully over the top of the cake, supporting it with a rolling pin, and position it so that it covers the cake (**B**). Using a smoother, smooth the top surface of the cake to remove any lumps and bumps. Smooth the top edge using the palm of your hand. Always make sure your hands are clean and dry with no traces of cake crumbs before smoothing sugarpaste.

4 Using a cupped hand and an upward movement, encourage the sugarpaste on the sides of the cake to adjust to the shape of your cake (**C**). Do not press down on any pleats in the paste, instead open them out and redistribute the paste, until the cake is completely covered. Smooth the sides using a smoother.

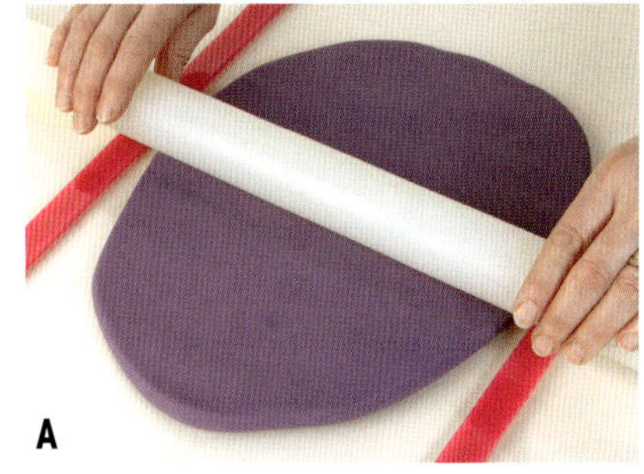

A

B

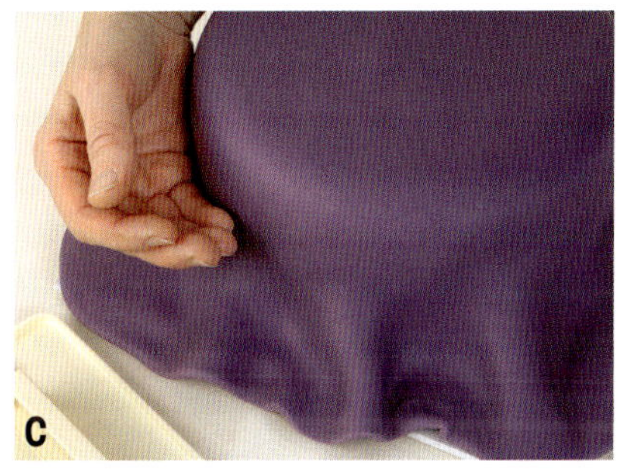

C

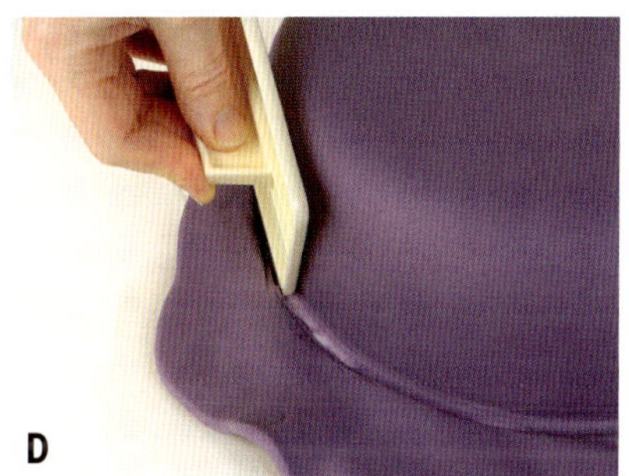

D

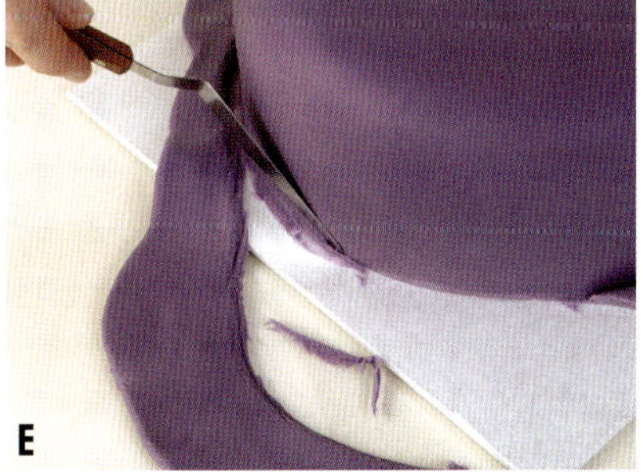

E

F

5 Take the smoother and while pressing down, run the flat edge around the base of the cake to create a cutting line (**D**). Trim away the excess paste with a palette knife (**E**) to create a neat, smooth edge (**F**).

"

Covering boards

Covering a board with sugarpaste gives you a canvas on which to add decoration to complement and enhance your cake design.

1 Roll out the sugarpaste to a thickness of 4mm (⅛in) or 5mm (³⁄₁₆in) using spacers.

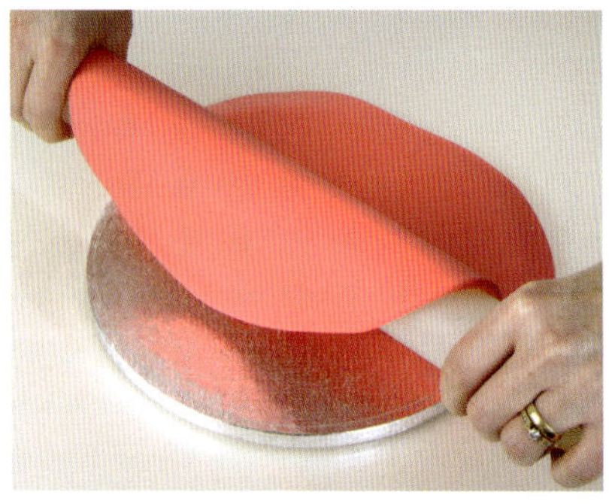

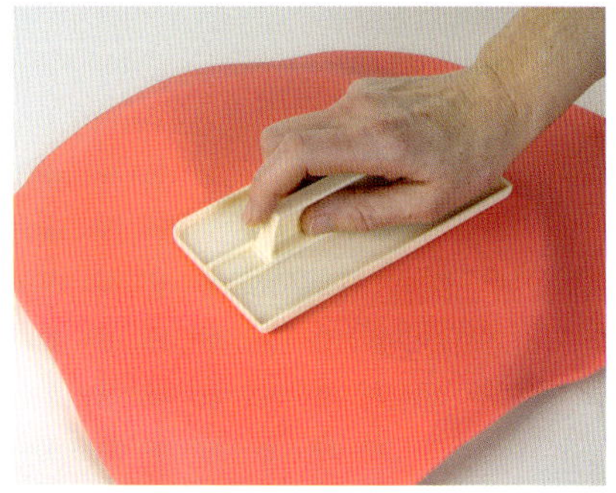

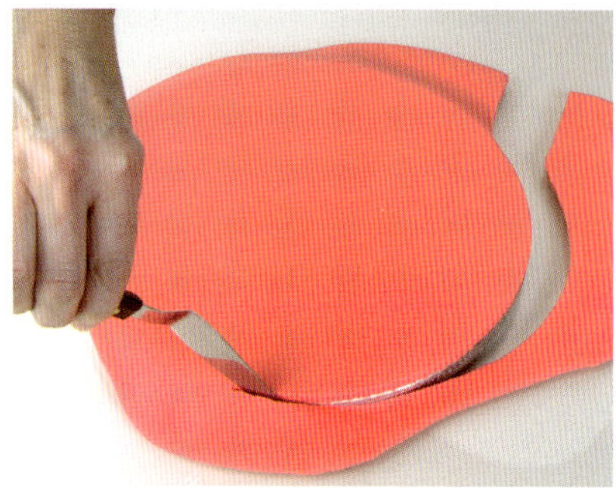

2 Moisten the board with cooled boiled water or sugar glue. Lift up the paste and drape over the board.

3 Circle a smoother over the paste to achieve a smooth, flat finish to the board.

4 Cut the paste flush with the sides of the board using a cranked handled palette knife, taking care to keep the edge vertical. The covered board should ideally be left overnight to dry thoroughly.

Covering the board and its sides

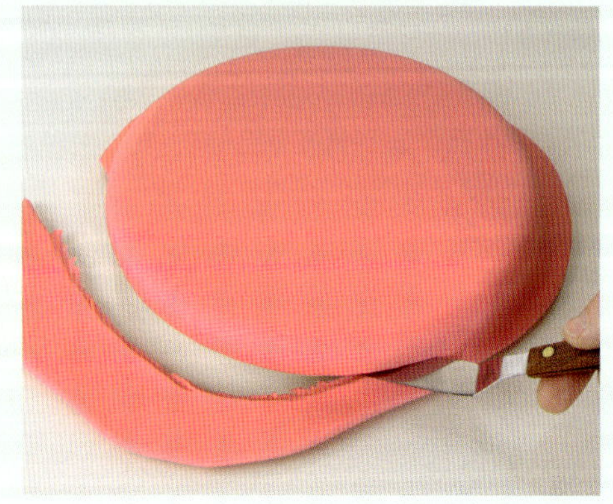

To cover a cake board plus its sides, as seen on the Coral Creation cake firstly place the cake board on a smaller board to lift it off your work surface. Roll out some sugarpaste and place it over the board. Take a smoother and using a circular motion smooth the paste to give a level surface, smooth the curved edge using the palm of your hand. Using a cranked handled palette knife, trim the sugarpaste flush with the underside of the board, taking care to keep the cut horizontal. Set aside to dry.

Covering mini-cakes

Mini-cakes are covered in exactly the same way as standard cakes, it is just the scale that is different. You will find that the icing pleats more readily so remember to keep opening the pleats (**A**) before smoothing to shape (**B**). You may also find that the sugarpaste is thicker at the bottom of the cake than the top – to help overcome this problem, rotate the cake between to two flat-edged smoothers to help redistribute the paste and ensure the sides of the cake are vertical (**C**).

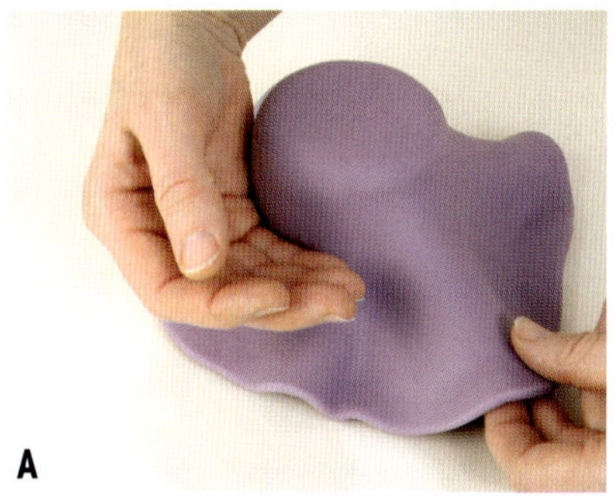

A

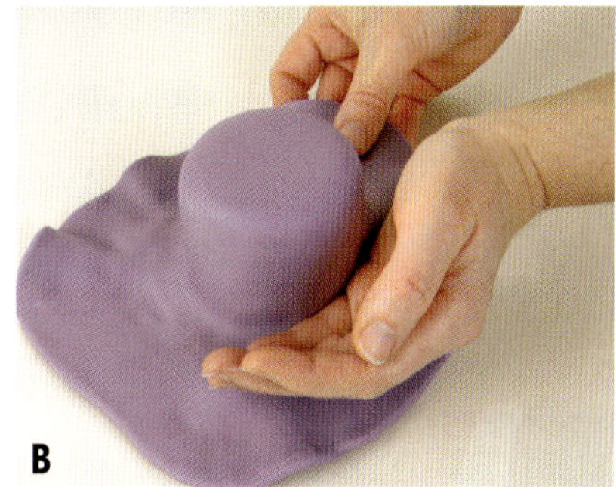

B

C

Using a sugar shaper

This is a fantastic tool – also often known as a clay gun, sugarcraft gun or craft gun The patented pump action of the sugar shaper gives mechanical assistance to squeeze out pastes in various shapes and sizes.

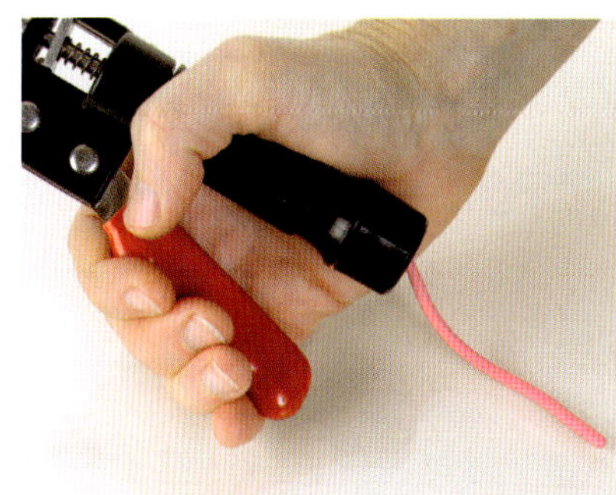

1 Add a little white vegetable fat (shortening) to the paste to stop it getting too sticky (note if too much is added the paste will not harden). Dunk the paste into some cooled boiled water and knead. Repeat until the paste feels soft and stretchy.

2 Insert the softened paste into the barrel of the sugar shaper, then add the required disc and reassemble the tool.

3 Push the plunger down to expel the air and pump the handle to build up pressure, until it 'bites'. The paste should squeeze out easily and smoothly – if it does not the consistency is probably incorrect so remove the paste and add some more fat (shortening) and/or water.

Covering cupcakes

It is worth doing a little preparation before covering your cupcakes. Not all cupcakes come out of the oven perfect, some may need a little trimming with a sharp knife while others benefit from a little building up with an appropriate icing.

1 Check each of your cupcakes to ensure that the decoration is going to sit just as you want it to and remedy any that aren't quite right.

2 The sugarpaste may need a little help to secure it to the cupcakes, so brush the cakes with an appropriate syrup or alcohol or add a thin layer of buttercream or ganache, this also adds flavour and interest to the cakes.

3 Knead the sugarpaste until warm and pliable. Roll out on a surface lightly smeared with white vegetable fat (shortening), rather than icing (confectioners') sugar. Roll out the paste to a depth of 5mm (³⁄₁₆in). It is a good idea to use spacers for this, as they ensure an even thickness.

4 Cut out circles of sugarpaste using an appropriately sized cutter. The size of the circle required will be dependant on the cupcake pan and case used and the amount the cakes have domed.

5 Using a palette knife, carefully lift the paste circles onto each cupcake. Use the palm of your hand to shape the paste to the cupcake, easing the fullness in if necessary.

Covering cookies

Sugarpaste is an excellent and very versatile medium for cookie decoration as it allows you to be extremely creative.

1 Smear white vegetable fat (shortening) over your work surface to prevent the icing sticking. Knead the sugarpaste to warm before use.

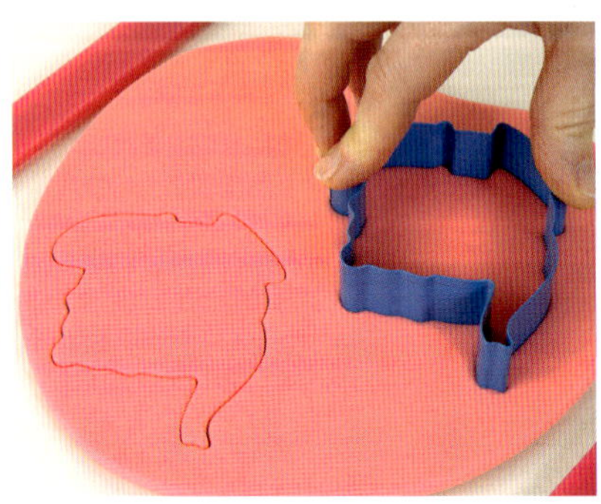

2 Roll out the kneaded sugarpaste to a thickness of 5mm (³⁄₁₆in) and cut out a shape using the same cookie cutter used to create the cookie. Remove the excess paste.

3 Paint piping gel over the top of the baked cookie to act as glue. Alternatively use buttercream or boiled jam.

4 Carefully lift the sugarpaste shape using a palette knife to prevent distorting the shape and place on top of the cookie. If the cookie cutter has left a ragged edge around the base of the shape, just carefully tuck this under with a finger before placing on the cookie.

5 Run a finger around the top cut edge of the sugarpaste to smooth and curve it.

Stacking Cakes

A multi-tiered cake, like a building, needs a structure hidden within it to prevent it from collapsing. It is important that this structure is 'built' correctly to take the loads put upon it, so follow these instructions carefully, as it is worth the time involved to get this stage correct.

Dowelling the cakes

All but the top tier will usually need dowelling to provide support.

1 Place the cakes to be stacked on hardboard cake boards of the same size as the cakes and cover each cake with sugarpaste, this ensures the boards are not visible yet gives the stacked cakes stability.

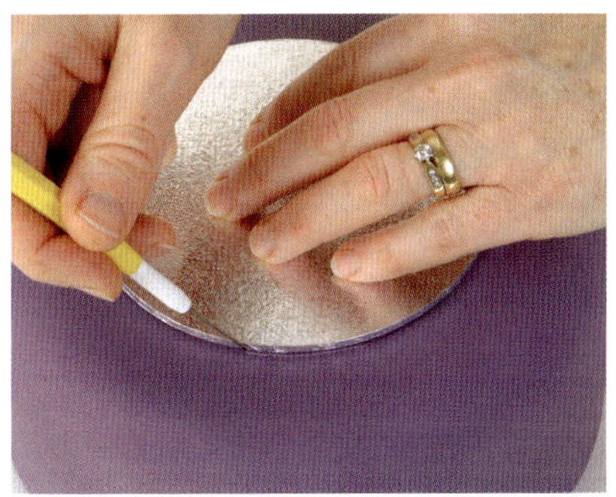

2 To support the cakes, dowels need to be inserted into all but the top tier. To do this, take the base cake and place a cake board the same size as the tier above in the centre of the cake. Scribe around the edge of the board to leave a visible outline.

3 Insert a dowel 2.5cm (1in) in from the scribed line vertically down through the cake to the cake board below. Make a knife scratch or pencil mark on the dowel to mark the exact height and remove the dowel.

4 Tape four dowels together. Then, using the mark on the inserted dowel, draw a pencil cutting line over the tape on the four dowels, making sure that the line is 90 degrees to the dowels (a set square helps). Next, using a small saw, such as a mitre saw that holds the dowels firm as it cuts, saw across the dowels.

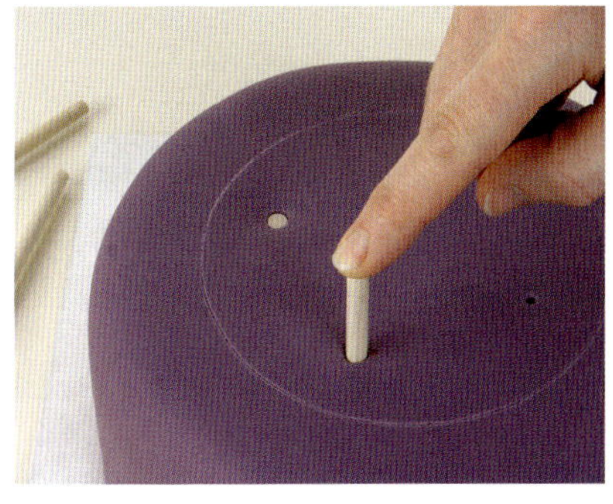

5 Place one of the dowels back in the measuring hole and insert the other dowels vertically down to the cake board at 3, 6 and 9 o'clock to the first one.

6 Repeat steps 1–5 for all but the top cake. It is essential that all the dowels are inserted vertically, are all the same length and have flat tops.

Stacking the cakes

Cover and dowel each cake before stacking. Place 15ml (1 tbsp) royal icing within the scribed area of the base cake and stack the next sized cake on top using the scribed line as a placement guide. Repeat the process with the remaining cakes.

Suppliers

Lindy's Cakes Ltd (LC)

Unit 2, Station Approach, Wendover
Buckinghamshire HP22 6BN
Tel: +44 (0)1296 622418
www.lindyscakes.co.uk
Online shop for products and
equipment used in this and Lindy's
other books, including Lindy's own
ranges of cutters and stencils

Abbreviations used in this booklet

DS – Designer Stencils

FI – First Impressions

FMM – FMM Sugarcraft

LC – Lindy's Cakes Ltd

PC – Patchwork Cutters

PME – PME Sugarcraft

SF – Sugarflair

W – Wilton

UK

Alan Silverwood Ltd
Ledsam House, Ledsam Street
Birmingham B16 8DN
Tel: +44 (0)121 454 3571
www.alansilverwood.co.uk
Manufacturer of multi-sized cake
pan, multi mini cake pans and
spherical moulds/ball tins

Ceefor Cakes
PO Box 443, Leighton Buzzard
Bedforshire LU7 1AJ
Tel: +44 (0)1525 375237
www.ceeforcakes.co.uk
Supplier of strong cake boxes –
most sizes available

FMM Sugarcraft (FMM)
Unit 7, Chancerygate Business
Park, Whiteleaf Road,
Hemel Hempstead, Hertfordshire
HP3 9HD
Tel: +44 (0)1442 292970
www.fmmsugarcraft.com
Manufacturer of cutters

Holly Products (HP)
Primrose Cottage, Church Walk,
Norton in Hales
Shropshire, TF9 4QX
Tel: +44 (0)1630 655759
www.hollyproducts.co.uk
Manufacturer and supplier of
embossing sticks and moulds

**M&B Specialised Confectioners
Ltd**
3a Millmead Estate, Mill Mead
Road
London N17 9ND
Tel: +44 (0)208 801 7948
www.mbsc.co.uk
Manufacturer and supplier of
sugarpaste

Patchwork Cutters (PC)
Unit 12, Arrowe Commercial Park,
Arrowe Brook Road, Upton
Wirral CH49 1AB
Tel: +44 (0)151 678 5053
www.patchworkcutters.co.uk
Manufacturer and supplier of
cutters and embossers

US

Global Sugar Art
625 Route 3, Unit 3
Plattsburgh, NY 12901
Tel: 1-518-561-3039 or 1-800-420-6088 (toll
free)
www.globalsugarart.com
Sugarcraft supplier that imports many UK
products to the US

Cake Craft Shoppe
3530 Highway 6
Sugar Land, TX 77478
Tel: 1-281-491-3920
www.cakecraftshoppe.com
Sugarcraft supplier

First Impressions Molds
300 Business Park Way, Suite A-200
Royal Palm Beach, FL 33411
Tel: 1-561-784-7186
www.firstimpressionsmolds.com
Manufacturer and supplier of moulds

Australia

Iced Affair
53 Church Street
Camperdown NSW 2050
Tel: +61 (0)2 9519 3679
www.icedaffair.com.au
Sugarcraft supplier